ABOUT THE AUTHOR

Greg Moodie is the cartoonist at *The National*, Scotland's newest daily newspaper. He is the author of three collections of cartoons, *Greg Moodie Versus The Union*, *Election Dissection* and *Striptease*, as well as *Borrowing Burns*, a semi-fictional or 'factually dubious' account of the making of his series of Tam O' Shanter murals.

Technically Dundonian, he graduated in Fine Art from the city's Duncan of Jordanstone College of Art sometime before the invention of fire, but believes that, like Vegas, what happened there stayed there.

He has written two novels, *The Unbearable Stupidity Of Being* and *Six Degrees Of Stupidity*, which he would dearly like to see in print before he dies, as he's unlikely to try anything so foolhardy again.

He currently resides in the Torphichen Free Republic (population 570), a conservation village and island state in Hidden West Lothian.

COOL SCOTS
Greg Moodie

Luath Press Limited

EDINBURGH

www.luath.co.uk

First published 2018

ISBN: 978-1-912147-20-5

The author's right to be identified as author of this book
under the Copyright, Designs and Patents Act 1988 has
been asserted.

The paper used in this book is recyclable. It is made from
low chlorine pulps produced in a low energy, low emission
manner from renewable forests.

Design and layout by Greg Moodie.

Printed and bound by Gomer Press, Llandysul

INTRODUCTION

There is an old Scottish saying: Some are born cool, some achieve coolness, and some have coolness thrust upon them. At least I think it's Scottish. It doesn't matter. The point is, there is no shortage of cool in Scotland, and narrowing it down to 42 exemplary individuals has taken a great deal of graft and some heated debate at the Torphichen Inn. Best buckle up.

In 2016, I produced a series of murals at said hostelry (they didn't ask me to, I did it when they weren't looking), based on the Robert Burns poem, 'Tam O' Shanter'. With six panels complete and no idea what to do with the seventh, long-suffering landlord Mr Kenny spotted my handiwork and suggested a portrait of the artist. I was flattered that he would welcome my permanent presence on the tavern wall as well as my permanent presence at the bar. He said he meant Burns, and declared loudly to the Torphy throng that I was a dullard of the highest standing. I was touched.

I agreed to do his bidding, and believe he was expecting tartan, heather, and all the other things you only ever see on the Royal Mile. But the following week, when I revealed my psychedelic *Beano*-wielding Burns, I nevertheless sensed that he was pleased. At least after the initial fainting and hysteria.

Several days passed and a recuperating Mr Kenny had received feedback from The Village People, the bleary-eyed residents of the Torphichen Free Republic.

'They say it's 'cool',' he offered hesitantly. 'What does that mean?'

'It means it's a work of unparalleled splendour,' I replied. 'You're very lucky to have made the boozy acquaintance of the genius behind it.' He seemed confused, but that's a default state in this part of the world.

It got me thinking. If a single Cool Scot could cause a stocky bald man to lose consciousness, imagine the impact of a series. I set about compiling a list, trying to limit the number of beards and old blokes who appear on teatowels. That's when it struck me. Scots may have invented the entire world, even discovered parts of space, but according to the history books, they were all guys.

That's right slackers, the story of Cool Scots is the story of men doing great things and being applauded, and women doing great things and being ignored. Or women being written out of history. Or women having to fight for things we now take for granted, like the right to vote or attend university. As I discovered, cool Scottish women in history are plentiful – you just probably don't know most of them yet.

'Men, women, living, dead, Scots spanning the best part of a millennium,' said my publisher, who, whilst a deviant of note, is mercifully clean-shaven. 'How do you plan to present this discovery?'

'Cool is timeless,' I replied. 'I shall pluck each of my subjects out of history and depict them in the hipster style of my choosing.' He looked at me askance and threw back his Absinthe.

The longlist became a shortlist. The shortlist became a shorter list, and that became the gem that you're currently reading over someone's shoulder. Not a definitive cool grouping by any means, but one that Scots can be proud of, and presented here in an order deliberately designed to jolt your feeble brains out of their preconceived ideas of time.

Celebrate the achievement. Marvel at the bravery. Shed a tear at the heartbreak and tragedy.

Try not to faint.

Greg Moodie, December 2017

CONTENTS

ALEXANDER GRAHAM BELL

(1847–1922)

Scientist and inventor

At first glance, it may seem odd that the person most closely associated with the invention of the telephone should have devoted the majority of his professional life to working with the deaf. But hey, that's just the sort of complexity that makes Scots so cool. You'll get used to this sort of thing as we go on.

Born in Edinburgh plain Alexander Bell ('Graham' was an 11th birthday gift from his father after young Bell's plea to have a middle name like his two siblings. Clearly the family had some social standing, as in those days only the wealthy could afford middle names), Bell's father and grandfather were elocutionists, and both his mother and wife were deaf.

At the age of 23, Bell emigrated to Canada, then to the USA, and developed a system called Visible Speech for teaching deaf children. He was fascinated by all aspects of speech and began conducting experiments into transmitting it, although being amongst Americans, it's hard to see what kept him motivated.

By 1875, Bell had developed a basic receiver that could turn electricity into sound and applied to have the device patented. Others had been conducting similar experiments at the time and there is considerable debate as to who correctly filled in the patent form first.

Thus began Bell's latter-day career as a court appearancee. It was an unfortunate situation given that the only thing worse than dealing with Americans is dealing with lawyers, and needless to say, dealing with American lawyers really is the pits.

It's telling that in later life Bell considered the telephone a nuisance and refused to have one in his study. But generations of teens would attest to the greatness of the invention, even if ironically their fascination with it might be contributing to the art of conversation's decline.

Coolness rating: Too cool for America

WILLIAMINA FLEMING

(1857–1911)

Astronomer

Born in Dundee, Williamina Stevens (known as Mina due to collective inability to correctly spell anything with three 'i's in it) had a short-lived marriage to a James Fleming, with whom she emigrated to Boston, Massachusetts, aged 21. When the wastrel Fleming scarpered, leaving her with child, Williamina found work as a housemaid, and in an unusual stroke of good fortune, her employer happened to be Edward Pickering, director of the Harvard College Observatory.

Even more unusually, Pickering was a progressive thinker and an advocate of higher education for women. Tiring of his beardy assistant's slacker attitude to work and his constant refrain of 'what's your star sign?', he said his Scottish maid could do a better job, even without chinwear, and to prove it, decided to train up young Mina. Soon she had traded the laundry for a telescope, a deal that was generally agreed to have worked in her favour, as laundry sucks.

By 1890, not only had she classified 10,351 stars into the newly created Pickering-Fleming System, she had made the discovery for which she is best known, the Horsehead Nebula, part of the constellation Orion, approximately 1,500 light years from Tayside. It's thought that the nebula had existed for a few years before this point but nonetheless it was an astonishing achievement, especially for a Dundonian.

Fleming proved so impressive that her employer put her in charge of hiring a team of women to study a burgeoning collection of star spectra photographs and take charge of all the observatory's publications. Over the course of the following 20 years she helped to shape astronomy into a scientific profession where women were taken seriously; one in which mansplaining was not so much frowned upon as laughed out of the room.

Coolness rating: Astronomically cool

ROBERT BURNS

(1759–1796)

Poet and lyricist

Widely regarded as Scotland's national poet, Robert Burns was a farmer's son who grew up in poverty in Alloway, Ayrshire. The young Burns experienced more than his fair share of hard manual labour and it's entirely understandable that he would soon want to turn his attention to poetry, drink and women at the earliest available opportunity. I know I would.

His first published collection of verse made him famous across the country and set out many of the themes which would go on to dominate his work: Scottish identity, poverty, egalitarianism, and the wonders of being an Olympic-standard debaucher. Almost as famous for his carousing and sexual relationships as for his work, Burns was untroubled by contemporary ideas of morality and even today would probably be referred to colloquially as a 'dirty shagger'.

Amongst the best-known works to spring from his prolific pen are 'To a Mouse', 'A Red Red Rose', 'Auld Lang Syne', and the long-form narrative poem, 'Tam O' Shanter'. Burns scholars tend to downplay his association with *The Merry Muses Of Caledonia*, a notorious collection of bawdy verse, but I can't imagine why. 'Short and thick, does the trick' is the most wonderful couplet.

Though he chiefly wrote in the Scottish dialect, his work transcends international boundaries and continues to inspire Burns clubs and societies around the world, as well as musicians and performers. His birthday, January 25th, is still celebrated each year with poetry, songs, whisky and haggis, which is quite delicious despite what's in it.

Burns crammed more into his 37 years than most of us could in several lifetimes. Amongst his last recorded words were 'I have not been idle', a phrase which, in terms of understatement, takes some beating.

Coolness rating: Red hot cool

MARGARET MACDONALD
(1864–1933)
Artist and designer

Margaret Macdonald was born near Wolverhampton, but in 1890 her Glasgow-born father, a colliery manager, brought the family back to his home town. There, on the cooler side of Hadrian's Wall, she and her sister Frances enrolled in Glasgow School of Art, studying design.

It was here that the sisters met their future husbands, James McNair and Charles Rennie Mackintosh. They became known as the Glasgow Four due to the limited imagination of those doing the naming. Had there been six of them, who knows what wonderfully witty appellation they could have landed.

The Four worked closely together, collaborating extensively and no doubt having the most rip-roaring carry-on. You know how those art students are. Sheesh. I remember this one time. Ach well.

Using watercolour, metalwork, embroidery and textiles, Margaret amassed an impressive body of work in a most distinctive style, often referred to as Art Nouveau, the Modern Style, or just the Glasgow Style. Personally I prefer The Spook School, a name used by the group's critics in reference to the gaunt, ghoulish figures in their work. I mean, who wouldn't want to be part of The Spook School?

Many of Macdonald's best known pieces were created for tearooms, a Victorian phenomenon that took off in the wake of the Temperance Movement. I shudder at the association, but I believe at the time these were hipster establishments where Cool Scots went to play, so I will make allowances.

Not unusually, Margaret's work has been overshadowed by that of her more famous husband's. But this is likely to be an issue to take up with critics and historians rather than artists. CRM himself said 'Margaret has genius, I have only talent', proving the age old saying that behind every successful man is a hack eager to overlook the work of his wife.

Coolness rating: Spookily cool

IVOR CUTLER

(1923–2006)

Poet, songwriter and humorist

For anyone unfamiliar with Ivor Cutler, no amount of wordage is likely to give an even halfway accurate account of this genuine one-off talent. Cutler's dry humour and deadpan delivery were uniquely Scottish and earned him admirers as diverse as Bertrand Russell, the Beatles and John Lydon. Which is pretty diverse.

Born in Glasgow to a Jewish family of Eastern European descent, his austere upbringing became the inspiration for his best-known work, *Life in a Scotch Sitting Room Vol. 2* (there is no *Vol. 1*). Here he turned his child's-eye view of the world into a peculiar little art form that was timeless, poetic and very funny.

Two anecdotes give an insight into his personality. During the Second World War he was dismissed from the RAF for being too interested in clouds. Then in London, teaching music, drama and poetry to 7–11 year-olds, one class involved improvising a song about killing your siblings.

In the late 1950s, he began making regular appearances on BBC TV and radio, often accompanying himself on harmonium. Paul McCartney was a fan and invited him to appear in the Beatles' *Magical Mystery Tour*, along with the Bonzo Dog Doo-Dah Band. I imagine teabreaks must have been pretty interesting.

In 1969 he recorded the first of many sessions for the John Peel show, where his absurdist humour chimed well with a generation familiar with the Bonzos and Monty Python. Between then and 1991, Peel introduced him to successive waves of new fans, who flocked to hear him perform his oddball songs about bugs, gruts and herrings ('Scotland gets its brains from the herrings').

A member of the Noise Abatement Society, Cutler cycled everywhere, could quote Homer, taught himself Chinese and often communicated through stickers adorned with Cutlerisms such as 'never knowingly understood'. His was indeed a beautiful cosmos.

Coolness rating: Cool and dry

MURIEL SPARK
(1918–2006)
Novelist

Spark was born Muriel Camberg in Edinburgh and attended James Gillespie's School for Girls, later the setting for her best-known book, *The Prime of Miss Jean Brodie*. After a failed marriage and a spell in Rhodesia, she relocated to London and in 1954 made the decision to join the Roman Catholic Church. Critics have suggested that her religious conversion was the central event of her life, but what do they know? It was probably just the one they found out about.

Certainly, Catholicism is a recurring theme in her work, beginning with 1957s *The Comforters*, a story about a woman who becomes aware she is a character in a novel. It's as well that Spark herself isn't around to become aware she is a character in *Cool Scots*, although I suspect her inherent coolness would allow her to overcome this indignity quite quickly.

In 1967, following the success of her early novels, Spark settled in Italy, a country which has been known to dabble in Roman Catholicism. There she developed her highly original writing style, making extensive use of imagined conversations in 'flash-forwards' – a technique I am familiar with, having been imagining chatting with her legal representatives.

As well as writing over 20 novels, Spark wrote poetry, short stories and critical studies of Mary Shelley and Emily Brontë, amongst others. But she also found time to fall out with her only son Robin, apparently over religion. It's thought to be one of the very few instances of people disagreeing on the subject.

Asked at one of her final public appearances in Scotland whether she would be seeing her Edinburgh-dwelling son, she allegedly replied 'I think I know how best to avoid him by now', a statement which, even by itself, would guarantee her a place amongst the coolest Scots of all time.

Coolness rating: The cool crème de la crème

JACKIE STEWART

(Born 1939)

Formula One racing driver

John Young Stewart is one of the great Formula One drivers from the golden era of the sport, a time before needless fripperies such as mandatory seatbelts and full-face helmets, and long before the introduction of extravagant, pointless on-track emergency services. Between 1965 and 1973, Jackie won three World Championships and was twice runner-up. Nothing could stop him. Even light was sluggish in comparison.

'The Flying Scot' was born in Milton, West Dunbartonshire, and started out as a mechanic in his car dealer father's garage. When a customer of the family business asked him to try out as a driver, 21-year-old Jackie had scored four wins before the customer even noticed. By 1964 he was driving in Formula Three and worked his way up the FS in minutes.

At his peak, Stewart held the record for most wins by a Formula One driver, but by 1973 had decided to retire. At the time, doctors were suggesting that regularly travelling at speeds in excess of 160mph could be considered a health hazard, and this may have influenced his decision.

He had a near miss in 1966 when his car left the track in heavy rain, leaving him trapped inside his overturned car for 25 minutes, soaked in fuel. There was no track crew, no doctor, no tools to get him out, and it took his team mates and a spanner borrowed from a spectator to free him. Subsequently, he began campaigning for greater safety measures in the sport and always taped a spanner to his steering shaft at every race. (The spectator was delighted to have played a minor role in the development of F1, but asked for his spanner back.)

Following retirement, Stewart became a successful F1 race commentator in the USA, Australia and Canada, where his unique insight and appealingly cool Scottish lilt made him a big hit amongst sports fans. Naturally he spoke unfeasibly fast.

Coolness rating: Cool, fast and furious

EVELINA HAVERFIELD

(1867–1920)
Suffragette and aid worker

Daughter of William Scarlett, the 3rd Baron Abinger, 'Evilena' Scarlett was born at Inverlochy Castle in the Highlands. Despite her birth name, she did not go on to become a major supervillain and instead spent a good deal of her life fighting for women's suffrage and helping Serbian war orphans. Blofeld was reportedly very disappointed in her.

Scarlett married a Royal Artillery officer, Major Henry Haverfield, and her comfortable lifestyle allowed her to pursue pastimes that were not yet mainstream for women, such as riding and cycling. She aligned herself with some of the moderate women's suffrage groups, only to find that moderation, in the face of being denied a vote, was overrated. Soon she was supporting militant suffragettes and taking a more hands-on approach to equal rights – by demonstrating regularly and punching the odd policeman.

She was arrested several times for interfering with the filth, most notably in 1910 when, as part of a Women's Social and Political Union demo, she whacked an officer in the mouth. She reportedly said: 'It was not hard enough. Next time I will bring a revolver.' Which goes to show, you should never mess with a cyclist.

At the outbreak of war in 1914, Haverfield founded the Women's Emergency Corps to train women to become doctors, nurses and motorbike couriers, and joined the Scottish Women's Hospital Units in Serbia, where the whole mess was really kicking off. By 1916 however, she was forced home – even the formidable Haverfield was unable to hold off the German advance.

Sensing a humanitarian crisis after the war's end, Haverfield returned to Serbia and established an orphanage in the mountain village of Bajna Bašta. She devoted herself to the children of the region and was working there when she caught pneumonia and died. The whole village turned out for her funeral, a cool Scot with a warm heart and a healthy intolerance for the world's nonsense.

Coolness rating: Militant cool

JAMES CLERK MAXWELL
(1831–1879)
Scientist

A pioneer in the field of mathematical physics, if it weren't for Maxwell's research into electromagnetic radiation we probably wouldn't have television or mobile phones. I imagine there have also been useful applications of his work. Maxwell was a true groundbreaker and simply years ahead of his time – it's only now that we're seeing the full flowering of the beardy hipster look.

Born in Edinburgh, the son of advocate John Clerk, his father inherited a 1,500-acre Galloway estate from his grandmother Dorothea Clerk-Maxwell, taking her name but declining the hyphen, as in those days hyphens required a permit. Young James Clerk Maxwell displayed an early, unquenchable thirst for knowledge, and when he first arrived at school sporting a tunic and a Galloway accent, his classmates knew they were dealing with someone special. They called him 'dafty'.

He seemed awfully bright for a dafty, writing his first scientific paper at the age of 14, then going on to university in Edinburgh and Cambridge. He became Professor of Physics at Aberdeen University aged 25 and began studying the composition of Saturn's rings. Up to that point, nobody had asked the obvious question: why don't they bump into each other?

By 1871, Maxwell had developed a unified theory of electromagnetism, which became known as Maxwell's Equations. Allow me to explain this to you now:

Aye, right.

But Einstein understood it, and said his own theory of relativity owed its origins to this work.

In the 1980s, the Voyager space probes showed that Saturn's rings remained stable due to being made up of countless small particles, each orbiting the planet independently – just as Maxwell predicted over a hundred years earlier.

Coolness rating: Unquenchably cool

JOAN EARDLEY

(1921–1963)
Artist

J oan Eardley was a painter whose work focused on two quite distinct subjects: the children of the streets around Townhead in Glasgow, and the blustery landscape of the remote Aberdeenshire fishing village, Catterline. She must have been a hardy and determined individual to have ventured out there day after day with her paint and canvases in such trying circumstances. I mean, children can be quite difficult.

Born in Warnham, Sussex, to dairy farmer parents, the family moved to Glasgow in 1939 just in time for it to be bombed. But the following year, Eardley enrolled in Glasgow School of Art and decided the bombed look suited her fine. She made her home amongst the condemned Townhead tenements, where ambitious city planners envisaged a brave new modernist world of motorway interchanges and underpasses. Luckily they ran out of money before anyone had to tell them to bugger off.

Eardley then trained as a teacher but didn't pursue the profession as, although she was quite comfortable working with children, she hadn't counted on other teachers.

Sometime in the early 1950s, she had the good fortune to contract mumps. Not normally a cause for celebration, but it was whilst convalescing that a friend took her to Catterline and showed her the North Sea. So taken was she with the sight that the artist began dividing her time between the two locations, and in 1954 bought a cottage in the village. They called it a cottage but it had no electricity, running water or sanitation. It was more of a box really.

By the time of her death, aged just 42, Eardley had quietly chalked up a body of work that left most of her contemporaries standing. Had her artistic career lasted more than its meagre 15 years, one can only imagine the full extent of her coolness.

Coolness rating: Wildly cool

JOHN MARTYN
(1948–2009)
Musician

One of the most important and influential singer-songwriters of the 20th century, John Martyn combined a unique impressionistic vocal style with emotionally raw material and achieved the unimaginable: he made folk music sexy. On hearing breakthrough 1973 album *Solid Air*, folkies everywhere cast off their bobbly jumpers and embraced a hitherto unknown world of sensual abandon. Many didn't even complain about the lack of harmonica.

Born Iain McGeachy in New Malden, Surrey, Martyn's parents were both opera singers. But even these difficult conditions didn't dent his enthusiasm for music. Having attended school in his father's native Glasgow following his parents' divorce, he soon headed south and established himself as one of the key performers in London's thriving folk scene.

'I've never been the Morris dancing type,' he said of that strange tank-topped world, and as if to prove it, he plugged in an Echoplex and introduced elements of jazz and rock, hitting a rich creative seam through the 1970s that culminated in *Grace And Danger*. But at the same time, he was becoming known as much for his drunken brawling and marital disharmony as his music. It's fair to say that his appetite for excess was not so much healthy as voracious.

He continued to produce quality recordings touched with moments of genius, but ongoing alcoholism and a self-destructive streak as wide as the Clyde made him an erratic performer. I personally attended a gig in which he seemed more intent on telling drummer jokes than singing. Whilst disconcerting, I had to admit his material was quite good.

Always one step away from major commercial success, Martyn nevertheless produced some of the most heartfelt, original and enduring music of the last 50 years. Face it, who else could bring a tear to your eye with the words 'May you never lose your temper if you get in a bar-room fight'?

Coolness rating: Excessively cool

MARY SOMERVILLE

(1780–1872)

Science writer

Often called the 'Queen of 19th Century Science', Mary Somerville gathered much of the leading scientific thinking of the period and turned it into something you might be able to read. She was also instrumental in the discovery of a large mass affecting the movement of the planet Uranus. It turned out to be Neptune, which until 1846 had been shy and not looking to cause any fuss.

In a reversal of the child prodigy scenario, 10-year-old Mary Fairfax could barely read or write, and when her vice admiral father returned from sea to their Burntisland home, he called her 'a savage'. Her response was not recorded, but she may have wondered who the Captain Pugwash was.

Mary was sent to an elite Musselburgh boarding school for a year and returned with some basic skills and a little French. She went on to study mathematics and astronomy, mostly alone, to the extent that her father, knowing a woman's constitution could not withstand intellectual rigour and she might go insane, tried to stop her. Luckily he died.

She married Samuel Grieg, an admiral in the Russian navy, who also took a dim view of women pursuing academic interests and agreed that study would warp his wife's tiny mind. Luckily he died too.

Her second husband, Dr William Somerville, was more useful. When Mary published 'The magnetic properties of the violet rays of the solar spectrum' for the Royal Society, he presented the paper – because naturally, women were not allowed to attend Royal Society meetings.

Somerville went on to translate Pierre Laplace's *Celestial Mechanics*, write the first geography text published in English, become the joint first female member of the Royal Astronomical Society and, in 2017, appear on a £10 note. She didn't even attend university.

Coolness rating: Polymathematically cool

R.D. LAING
(1927–1989)
Psychiatrist

C ontroversial headshrink Ronald David Laing spent his life challenging many of his profession's attitudes towards mental illness and decrying traditional methods of treatment. He wondered, for example, if sending electricity through patients' heads in order to make them feel better was such a great idea.

Born in Glasgow's Govanhill to decidedly odd parents (during pregnancy his mother wore an oversized coat in case anyone found out she'd had sex, and later made a voodoo doll of her son; his father had delicate mental health, possibly due to having a wife who made voodoo dolls of their son), Laing studied medicine at Glasgow University, probably just to get out of the house.

It was whilst treating schizophrenics as a British Army psychiatrist in the early 1950s that Laing began developing his radical theories. Amongst them, that madness isn't so bad, it just has poor PR; that a breakdown might be your best career choice at this point; and that it's not you that's sick, it's society – that is to say, it's everybody else's fault that you're mad. He also said schizophrenia was a theory, not a fact. But there are two sides to that story.

Following the publication of *The Divided Self* in 1960, Laing found himself much in demand. It may have been his preference for self-healing. It may have been his role in the anti-psychiatry movement. Or it may have been that he liked giving everybody LSD. Amongst those allegedly looking to be cured were The Beatles, Sean Connery and Van Morrison.

With such unorthodox methods and a turbulent personal life (he fathered ten children with four women, and struggled with alcoholism and depression), the General Medical Council always had him in their sights, and in 1987 he was forced to stop practising. Two years later he died of a heart attack whilst playing tennis in Saint-Tropez. Some suspected voodoo.

Coolness rating: Incurably cool

MARGO MACDONALD

(1943–2014)

Politician

An outspoken and charismatic politician, Margo MacDonald spent most of her professional life taking on challenging and complex issues, championing controversial causes and being a thorn in the side of opponents and her party leaders alike. A committed supporter of independence, she had a difficult relationship with the Scottish National Party. She was disciplined, expelled, everything short of fired out of a cannon before standing as an independent candidate for Lothian in 2003 – a seat she held until her death.

MacDonald grew up in Hamilton, South Lanarkshire, and trained as a physical education teacher, something which may have helped equip her for the vigours of a parliamentary career. Her first foray into politics was also her most stunning success. In the 1973 Govan by-election she won a shock victory for the SNP in what had been predominantly Labour territory since 1918. There were scenes of near-hysteria at the count as supporters realised they had elected not just a tireless and effective representative, but a particularly cool one.

Later, MacDonald said she had been approached by both KGB and CIA agents posing as journalists, that the SNP had been infiltrated by MI5 and, during the 2014 independence campaign, she wrote to the security services asking for assurances that they would stay out of it. It's possible that her fears were ungrounded, but just because you're paranoid doesn't mean the British state isn't monitoring your every bum sneeze. I bet they've already read this book.

A vocal campaigner for assisted suicide, she brought forward the End of Life Assistance Bill in 2010. It was an issue with personal resonance for MacDonald as she had been diagnosed with Parkinson's disease several years before. Despite polls showing widespread public support for the measure, the bill was defeated then and once again after her death. Had she survived, the matter is highly unlikely to have ended there.

Coolness rating: Too cool for your party

ANDREW CARNEGIE
(1835–1919)
Industrialist and philanthropist

Not so much 'rags to riches' as 'rags to wealth beyond the concept of numbers', Andrew Carnegie amassed a personal fortune that allowed him to consider retiring in his 30s – but by the time of his death he had given 90 per cent of it away.

Carnegie was born in a single-room cottage in Dunfermline, the son of a handloom weaver and a cobbler's assistant. When the impoverished young family got tired of being unable to all fit in the room at the same time, they decided to try their luck in the United States, and in 1848 moved to Allegheny, Pennsylvania. There, aged 13, Andrew got his first job in the cotton industry as a spool. I don't know, I may have picked that up wrong.

A bright young man, he thought working 12-hour shifts 6 days a week for low pay wasn't all it was cracked up to be, and progressed through a series of positions in the railway industry, learning about business practices and how not to be poor. The steel industry was where he cracked it, his Carnegie Steel Company having discovered more efficient methods of manufacturing the blue stuff. Soon he would need more than a single room just to store his money.

But realising it was pointless being the richest bloke in the morgue, he began devoting more of his time to philanthropy. Amongst his many projects, Carnegie funded 3,000 libraries in the USA, Canada, Ireland, Australia, New Zealand, South Africa, the West Indies, Fiji and… Dunfermline. That's a lot of libraries. Just think how much stupider we'd all have been without him.

And on the subject of stupid, Carnegie was also a lifelong critic of the monarchy, writing extensively on the subject long before we all realised that the British royals were a bunch of duds.

'There is little success where there is little laughter,' he said. I've been laughing all my life in the hope that a bit of his kind of success might show up.

Coolness rating: Steely cool

FLORA MACDONALD

(1722–1790)

Jacobite heroine

Adventure seemed to follow Flora MacDonald around, whether in Scotland, America or on the high seas in between. It most famously came knocking in the shape of Prince Charles Edward Stuart, or Bonnie Prince Charlie, in 1746. The beleaguered prince had just led the Jacobite rebellion, which frankly didn't go so well, and had been pursued by government forces as far as the island of Benbecula in the Outer Hebrides. Geographically, that's about as remote as you get in Scotland. Practically Iceland.

Twenty-four-year-old MacDonald helped the prince to escape the island by disguising him as her maid and sailing with him to Skye. In this way he avoided capture and was able to spend the rest of his days on the continent. It's not known how much he enjoyed the experience of being dressed as a maid, but his passage was immortalised in the 1884 'Skye Boat Song'.

After a short spell of incarceration in the Tower of London for this act of devilry, MacDonald emigrated to America only to get caught up in the War of Independence. Her husband fought on the side of the British and was captured by rebels, forcing Flora into hiding while their family plantation was looted. Subsequently, America floundered as an independent nation, just as the British government said it would, and has spent over 200 years begging to be recolonised.

In 1779 MacDonald decided to return to Scotland but, true to form, was caught up in a mid-Atlantic skirmish with a French privateer intent on taking the merchant ship as bounty. By now, her patience tested, she was not so much cool as frosty. She took a dim view of the assailants, refused to go below deck during fighting and was wounded as a result.

The renowned essayist and lexicographer Dr Samuel Johnson, who met MacDonald during his travels in the Western Isles, summed her up by saying she was 'just ridiculously hip'. Or something like that.

Coolness rating: Feistily cool

SEAN CONNERY

(Born 1930)

Actor

Widely regarded as Scotland's most famous son, Connery is at least its most famous former milkman, having driven a float around Fountainbridge, Edinburgh, as a young man. It was one of many jobs – lorry driver, lifeguard, artist's model, coffin polisher – that he took on whilst trying to break into acting. Who even knew coffin polishing was a thing?

He got that break in 1962 with the part of secret agent James Bond. However, Bond creator Ian Fleming was initially unsure about the casting, stating "he's not what I envisioned of James Bond looks". Given that Connery is 6'2", a former Mr Universe finalist, and still regularly tops 'Sexiest Man Alive' polls, one can only wonder about Fleming's standards.

Connery played Bond seven times and became synonymous with the character, but eventually grew tired of what he called 'the whole Bond bit'. I imagine being mistaken in the street for a glamorous spy who sips Martini and beds the world's most beautiful women could become wearisome.

He went in search of more challenging and intellectually stimulating movies, but unfortunately made *Zardoz* instead. On the plus side, vacating the Bond role gave Roger Moore something to do.

Nevertheless, the star status that Bond lent him ensured he was in constant demand, and a succession of high profile movies followed. He won an Oscar for *The Untouchables*, then went on to be Harrison Ford's dad in one of those films with the hats.

A lifelong supporter of Scottish independence, he became Sir Sean in 2000 after having tricked the British establishment into believing that a 70-year-old couldn't possibly be an upstart. He retired a few years later, once he realised that Hollywood was run entirely by bawheids. It was their loss, and ours. You don't get movie stars this big anymore.

Coolness rating: Over ice, shaken not stirred

ANNIE LENNOX
(Born 1954)
Musician and activist

Whilst best-known as a hugely successful singer/songwriter, Annie Lennox has also been a tireless campaigner for AIDS awareness, human rights and the eradication of poverty, supporting the work of organisations like Unicef, Amnesty, Greenpeace and the Red Cross, and being far less annoying than Bono.

Showing an early talent for music in her hometown of Aberdeen, the only Scottish city in which the word 'whereabouts' is pronounced 'furry boots' and framed as a question, Lennox secured a place at London's Royal Academy of Music where she studied flute, piano and harpsichord, the latter most likely inspired by Lurch from the Addams Family.

It was whilst in London that she first met long-time collaborator, guitarist Dave Stewart, who at the time had been developing innovative facial hair patterns and the occasional tune. As The Tourists, they had a couple of top 10 hits, but it was in 1980 when the duo left to start The Eurythmics that their creativity skyrocketed, and Stewart achieved the ultimate goatee.

The Eurythmics were one of the biggest pop acts of the '80s and Lennox, with her soaring, soulful vocals and striking looks, was the band's calling card. At one point they were selling so many records that the word 'gazillion' had to be invented. They were number one everywhere except Mars. But by the end of the decade, the eury sheen had worn off and Lennox went solo. Dave Stewart's facial hair also branched out.

Lennox's full history of charitable giving would need another book to document, one far less silly than this one. In 2013 Archbishop Desmond Tutu said of her: 'She is one of those exemplary human beings who chose to put her success in her chosen career to work in order to benefit others.' Furry boots? Mostly in Africa.

Coolness rating: The soul of cool

JOSEPH KNIGHT

(1750–unknown)
Slave

Sometimes referred to as the last slave in Scotland, 'Joseph Knight' was an African who had the misfortune to encounter the worst excesses of an unenlightened period in our history, but who, through intelligence and determination, effectively ended slavery here in Alba. The story reminds me of the line from the classic 1960s song, 'Born free, till some bastard caught me', though my memory for lyrics has never been great.

Born in Guinea, 12-year-old Knight was captured and taken to Jamaica, then a major hub for sugar production, and given the name of the ship's captain. In Jamaica he was bought at auction by Scottish landowner John Wedderburn who, even though he made Knight a houseboy rather than a regular field slave, would still put the cast of *Horrible Bosses* in the shade.

In 1769, Wedderburn returned to Perthshire, taking Knight with him. It wasn't so much the high temperatures and near-constant sunshine that bothered Knight, as a landmark case south of the border which ruled that slavery was not recognised in English Law. In response, Knight demanded freedom and back wages. Wedderburn, furious at the sheer ingratitude of a man he allowed to see to his every need without pay, had him thrown in jail.

Knight took his master to court, and for a black dude in 18th century Perth, that took some giant Guinean baws. But he had some heavyweight support from men of letters James Boswell and Samuel Johnson, and besides, the alternative was to continue wiping some knobby laird's backside. In 1777, after a series of verdicts and appeals, he was declared a free man and the principle of slavery was rejected in Scotland.

Little else is known about Knight. He trained as a barber in Dundee, married a woman who had also been in Wedderburn's service, and slipped quietly into obscurity. Given what he had been through, this may have suited him just fine.

Coolness rating: Determinedly cool

MARY BARBOUR

(1875–1958)
Political activist

Mary Barbour was behind one of the most successful examples of people power ever seen, organising a Govan women's group into a rent-striking force that made unscrupulous landlords shake in their gout-ridden boots. (Landlords are often subject to bad press and I'm delighted to be able to continue that noble tradition here.)

Following the outbreak of the First World War, thousands of workers converged on Glasgow's thriving shipyards and munitions factories. With call for housing at a peak, property owners raised rents in a 'supply and demand' idea apparently popular with capitalists. They also believed that with many of the men at war, their wives would put up little resistance. Unfortunately for them, one of the wives was Mary Barbour.

Mary Rough was born in Kilbarchan, Renfrewshire, and had settled in Govan with her shipyard engineer husband David Barbour. By 1915, women in the area were already protesting about living conditions, so when rents shot up and evictions began taking place, they were less than amused.

Their response was to form the South Govan Women's Housing Association, with Barbour at the helm. As well as advocating non-payment of rent increases, the group staged mass demonstrations and actively interfered with evictions, becoming known as 'Mrs Barbour's Army'. Landlords began to think they'd chosen the wrong battle.

By the end of 1915, with 20,000 tenants telling owners where to go, the government stepped in, halting legal actions and freezing all rents at pre-war levels. It was a rare moment of intelligence for an administration more used to dealing with Glaswegians by sending them off to die pointlessly in a muddy field.

Barbour went on to become one of Glasgow's first woman councillors, and I like to think that in this role she was a ballbreaker of some standing.

Coolness rating: Strikingly cool

ALASTAIR SIM
(1900–1976)
Actor

There is a plaque on the wall of the Edinburgh Filmhouse which says Alastair Sim was born 'near here'. It's the sort of vagueness that this very private man would have loved; somewhere in the vicinity, you don't really need to know.

Sim worked at his father's tailoring business in nearby Princes Street before announcing to his parents at the age of 18 that he wanted to become an actor. He may as well have said he wanted to be a drug dealer, or a cartoonist. Such was the fallout from this unholy declaration that he avoided treading the boards until the age of 30 and became an elocutionist instead. (To this day, cartooning enjoys a reputation on a par with shoplifting.)

Determined to be a disappointment to his parents, he began appearing in West End productions in the 1930s. But it was his film roles of the '40s and '50s which brought him fame. By turns sinister and comic, he was the perfect Ebenezer Scrooge and, when Margaret Rutherford was unavailable for *The Belles of St Trinian's*, he played the dual role of the headmistress and her shady brother.

Sim and his wife Isabella went to extremes to encourage struggling young talent, taking in a succession of actors like 15-year-old George Cole (later of *Minder* fame), who lived with them for 14 years. Suspicion and innuendo followed, and those doing the whispering must have been doubly incensed that such a public figure asked for privacy, rarely giving interviews and refusing to sign autographs. Of course, in the 21st century this sort of nurturing behaviour would be deemed unacceptable, as caring for the under-privileged and vulnerable is very much frowned upon.

In 1953 Sim was awarded a CBE, but two decades later he declined a knighthood, describing himself as a lifelong socialist and saying 'everyone is equal'. The whisperers must have had a field day.

Coolness rating: Enunciatingly cool

JESSIE KESSON
(1916–1994)
Novelist and playwright

Probably the coolest Scot to have been born in a workhouse, Jessie Kesson overcame the most appallingly adverse conditions to become a highly-acclaimed author and radio producer. Workhouses — forced, unpaid labour for the poor — were formally abolished in 1930, but the current British government is hoping to bring about a revival.

Born Jessie McDonald in Inverness, she was removed from her mother's care at the age of eight and raised in an orphanage at Skene, Aberdeenshire. She showed great promise at school but was denied further education, as it was generally agreed that a pauper girl's time is best spent drudging.

Jessie married farm worker Johnnie Kesson in 1937 and the couple toiled together in various agricultural jobs. She began writing in her spare time and in 1945 created her first BBC radio play. Relocating to London, she would go on to write around 100 plays and become a producer of *Women's Hour*, a radical idea that allowed women to not only have views, but to express them.

It was the golden age of radio, and the BBC was known for its handsome fees; Kesson was so well-paid that she was able to take on second jobs in a hospital, a cinema, a Woolworths store and an art college, where she posed nude for students.

Incredibly, she still found time to write several novels, using the raw material of her impoverished early years for 1958's *The White Bird Passes* and her experience of farm labouring for 1983's *Another Time, Another Place*. Critics suggested her period at Woolworths was probably not the best use of her time.

In the 1980s, Kesson was awarded honorary degrees by the University of Dundee and the University of Aberdeen, which I personally hope went some way to removing the heartbreaking sting of being denied a full education in her youth.

Coolness rating: A cool triumph over adversity

ALEX HARVEY

(1935–1982)

Musician

Teaming up with Glasgow heavy rock outfit Tear Gas in 1972 to form The Sensational Alex Harvey Band, Gorbals-born Harvey said the group were introverts onstage but extroverts offstage, and that this situation would need reversing. He certainly achieved his goal – throughout the '70s, SAHB live shows were the performance equivalent of a mugging.

Harvey was already a stage veteran. As a teenager he played guitar in various jazz and skiffle groups, and won a competition to find Scotland's answer to Tommy Steele. It may be hard to imagine this most Glaswegian of rock frontmen and the Lambeth cheeky chappy having much in common, but it's worth remembering that Scots are not only cool, they're versatile.

In 1960, Harvey and his Big Beat Band supported Johnny Gentle and His Group. As it turned out, Gentle's 'Group' were an early incarnation of The Beatles. Harvey then went on to find some success with The Big Soul Band, playing a bluesy rock and roll, and spending a sizeable chunk of the '60s on tour. It's not known what happened to The Beatles.

After four years as a rhythm guitarist in the London stage production of Hair, the 37-year-old finally found a suitable vehicle for his considerable talents. Drawing from burlesque and music hall traditions, SAHB recorded eight critically acclaimed albums in the six years to 1978. They even had a top ten hit with a cover version of 'Delilah', infusing the song with a disturbing but entirely appropriate comic menace that would likely keep Tom Jones awake at night.

A charismatic performer whose stage persona was part troubadour, part highwayman, Harvey was the personification of the great Scots word 'gallus'. When he died of a heart attack at the age of 47, the world was robbed of a sharp and insightful writer, and rock music became just that little bit less dangerous again.

Coolness rating: Sensationally cool

JACKIE KAY
(Born 1961)
Writer and poet

Jackie Kay is a multi-award-winning writer of poetry, fiction and drama, and the current Scots Makar; the Scottish Poet Laureate, for the uncool. (Originally, the Makars were a group of 15th and 16th century poets often referred to as Scots Chaucerians by literary critics, who would go to great lengths to avoid trying to pronounce the word Makar. It's 'macker', dullards.)

Kay was born to an Edinburgh mother and Nigerian father but she and her brother were adopted by a white Scots couple and raised in Bishopbriggs, Glasgow. Her adoptive father was a full-time employee of the Communist Party and her adoptive mother was the Scottish secretary of CND. There is a possibility that they had a left-leaning perspective, but at this stage it's just a hunch.

Initially Kay had planned to be an actress, but when god of literature Alasdair Gray read her poetry, he advised her to become a writer. I once asked Alasdair Gray if I should become a writer, but he didn't reply. I ended up doing this instead.

Kay's work deals with themes such as race, gender, identity and sexuality, and is often autobiographical. Her first book, *The Adoption Papers*, is told from the multiple viewpoints of a child, her mother and adoptive mother. Her novel *Trumpet* was inspired by the true story of a jazz musician who was discovered after his death to have been biologically a woman. A really parpy one.

In 2012, she became the first writer to read aloud a poem at a football stadium prior to kick-off. Given the reputation for drunken hooliganism, it was a daunting gig. But poets aren't nearly as badly behaved as they used to be.

Kay has lived in Manchester for some time, but says: 'You don't need to live in Scotland to be Scottish, to have the language, to have a Scottish heart and a Scottish sensibility. If anything, it can heighten those senses.' For Cool Scots, being Scottish is a state of mind.

Coolness rating: Identifiably cool

BILLY MACKENZIE
(1957–1997)
Singer

One of pop music's most colourful characters, Billy Mackenzie was the singer with The Associates whose distinctive operatic voice and flamboyant dress sense marked him and the group as one of the '80s' stand-out acts. An other-worldly figure who never quite gelled with the pop machine, he seemed most comfortable at home with his pet whippets and, given his multi-octave vocal range, it's likely there are tracks that only they could hear.

Mackenzie grew up listening to Sparks and David Bowie in his hometown of Dundee, teaming up with multi-instrumentalist Alan Rankine in 1976. Their first single was a cover of 'Boys Keep Swinging', released just weeks after Bowie's own version – an eccentric decision, but one that would bring record companies calling. When they later chose to sign with Warner Brothers, Mackenzie said it was because he liked Bugs Bunny.

In 1982, the band scored a top ten hit with the wonderfully deranged 'Party Fears Two', a song with one of the oddest opening lines ever: 'I'll have a shower and then phone my brother up'. Success was sweet. They moved into a London Holiday Inn, taking an additional room for Mackenzie's pets, who were fed room service smoked salmon. They didn't call it the decade of excess for nothing.

But already tiring of promotional responsibilities, Mackenzie backed out of a US tour, establishing a pattern of oddball behaviour that would continue throughout the rest of his career. Being dropped by a London record company in the '90s, he asked if they would call a contract cab to take him home. They duly obliged and Mackenzie drove the 500 miles back to Dundee.

Along with his extreme vocal talents, Mackenzie said he had 'an extreme repertoire of emotions'. Following the death of his mother and a bout of severe depression, he took an overdose of prescription medication and died, aged just 39. The phrase 'voice of an angel' was never more tragically apt.

Coolness rating: Cool in extremis

JAMES BARRY

(c.1790–1865)

Surgeon

Though not strictly Scottish, I believe James Barry, the first confirmed transgender medical doctor in the world, is, in the words of Muriel Spark, 'Scottish by formation'. Barry was born Margaret Bulkley in Cork, Ireland, and went on to become a pioneering military surgeon. (Some argue that Barry was the first woman to qualify as a doctor, by some 50 years, but as the young medical student presented as a man from matriculation till death, I'd suggest that was a pretty clear statement of intent.)

Margaret Bulkley's uncle was the renowned romantic painter James Barry. When he died, leaving the family a modest inheritance, Bulkley thought of a novel way of putting the old boy's cash to work. Opportunities for women to enter university were limited, in the sense that there were none, so the ambitious youngster took the artist's name and enrolled in Edinburgh University Medical School. The unbroken voice and soft features were put down to youth, and study proceeded without incident. It was unusual, but then look at Wee Jimmy Krankie.

Qualifying in 1812, Dr Barry went on to the Royal College of Surgeons in London and then joined the British Army in Cape Town, South Africa. Here, before anaesthetics and when amputation was common if you had so much as a headache, Barry began experimenting with new procedures and performed the first successful caesarean section.

The doctor was a success by any measure, and the biological reality remained unknown until after Barry's death, when it was revealed that the deceased was not only fully female, but had given birth.

This story is often told in terms of deception; that Barry 'fooled' the academics, the military, high society. But Barry showed up day after day, witnessed the most appalling casualties, and saved lives. If it was deception, it was in the face of an unjust and outdated system, and thousands benefited. Doctors are doctors.

Coolness rating: Transformatively cool

RIKKI FULTON

(1924–2004)
Comedian and actor

Rikki Fulton's best-known comic character, the dour, misnomered Reverend I.M. Jolly – whose memoirs were entitled *How I found God and why he was hiding from me* – could only have come from Alba. The Church of Scotland minister became a Hogmanay institution as part of Fulton's sketch series *Scotch and Wry*, running from 1978 to 1993. Only once, in 1983, was the show screened south of the border, after which it was agreed it was too cool for England.

Born Robert Kerr Fulton, his family ran a stationer's shop in Dennistoun, Glasgow. After being discharged from the Royal Navy, where he had been part of the D-Day Coastal Forces, Rikki joined the family business whilst also working as a straight actor in repertory theatre. In what was surely a first, acting turned out to be the more stable of the two professional environments, and Fulton chose to concentrate on the stage. He moved to London and became the smooth-talking compère of the BBC's *Showband Show*.

Back in Scotland, he began performing in pantomime and summer revues and it was here that he teamed up with comedian Jack Milroy to form the stage double act 'Francie and Josie'. Translated to the small screen in the 1960s, it's thought to have been the only Glaswegian teddy boy sitcom in history.

At the same time as his comedy roles, Fulton also notched up substantial stage and screen credits as a serious actor. He performed in various adaptations of Molière, was Autolycus in a BBC production of Shakespeare's *The Winter's Tale* and played a KGB agent in the 1983 film *Gorky Park*. But admit it, you'd probably rather hear about Supercop.

A highly original talent, it's hard to think of anyone else who could have taken Molière's *Le Bourgeois Gentilhomme* and created a hit Edinburgh Festival production called *A Wee Touch o' Class*.

Coolness rating: Cool and wry

WINNIE EWING
(Born 1929)
Politician

Winnie Ewing is the only politician to have been a member of the Westminster parliament, the Scottish parliament and the European parliament. As well as being a tireless campaigner for Scottish interests, she is clearly also a glutton for punishment.

Born Winifred Woodburn in Glasgow, she joined the pro-independence Student Nationalists while training as a solicitor at Glasgow University. She went on to practise law and it was not until 1967 that Woodburn saw the error of her ways. That year, she was encouraged to stand as a candidate for the Scottish National Party in the Hamilton by-election, a safe Labour seat since the ice age.

In what turned out to be a pivotal moment in Scottish politics, Ewing romped home with 46 per cent of the vote, a swing of nearly 38 per cent from Labour. When the victory was declared, Ewing famously said 'Stop the world, Scotland wants to get on'. Scotland has been trying to get on ever since, but the British establishment would generally prefer that it stayed off.

Ewing was one of only 26 female MPs at the time and, as if overcoming prejudice wasn't hard enough in the staunchly male corridors of power, she also wanted to take Scotland out of the United Kingdom. She felt as welcome as scurvy, but her time there saw SNP membership increase significantly.

As a member of the European parliament between 1975 and 1999, Ewing earned the nickname 'Madame Ecosse'. It was intended as an insult, but Ewing embraced it – Cool Scots have a way of turning these things to their advantage. She only gave up the position in order to become a member of the Scottish parliament in its first session.

As the oldest sitting MSP, it was Ewing's duty to formally open the Holyrood parliament in 1999. 'The Scottish Parliament, adjourned on the 25th day of March in the year 1707, is hereby reconvened,' she said, to great relief all round.

Coolness rating: World-stoppingly cool

ROBERT LOUIS STEVENSON
(1850–1894)
Novelist

Hugely successful during his lifetime and now one of the world's most widely-translated authors, Stevenson's work was all but written off as second-rate genre fiction after his death. Budding novelists should learn from this and always create difficult and obscure work that nobody reads, as people don't take you seriously when you sell tsunami-loads of books.

Originally Robert 'Lewis' Stevenson, he changed the spelling of his middle name to save characters, before realising it was a false economy. He was on the verge of changing it back when everyone started calling him RLS, and that nailed the whole issue to everyone's satisfaction.

When the 23-year-old Stevenson, son of a respected Edinburgh lighthouse engineer, grew his hair long, started wearing velveteen Jimi Hendrix tunics (at the time, Hendrix was little known outside London), renounced Christianity, and declared his intention to become a writer, his parents took it well. 'You have rendered my whole life a failure,' said his father. 'This is the heaviest affliction that has ever befallen me,' said his mother. It's possible that the subsequent success of *Treasure Island*, *Kidnapped* and *The Strange Case of Dr Jekyll and Mr Hyde* may have altered this viewpoint, but who knows. Some parents are never happy until you become an accountant.

Stevenson suffered from bronchial ill health throughout his life and travelled extensively in search of suitable recuperative environments. Eventually he settled in Samoa and took the native name 'Tusitala', which is Samoan for 'Sickboy'.

Despairing of his physical condition and fearing permanent invalidity, he railed: 'I wish to die in my boots; no more Land of Counterpane for me. To be drowned, to be shot, to be thrown from a horse.' In the end, he died whilst chatting with his wife and grappling with a bottle of wine, which, let's face it, is a much cooler way to go.

Coolness rating: A cool treasure

VICTORIA DRUMMOND
(1894–1978)
Marine engineer

The first woman to become a chief engineer in the Merchant Navy and the first woman member of the Institute of Marine Engineers, Drummond spent her 40-year career doing the same hard physical engine room work as her male counterparts, but with the added task of continually explaining to immediate superiors how being an engineer and a woman was possible. Even with charts and diagrams, many remained baffled.

Born at Megginch Castle, Perthshire, her father Captain Malcolm Drummond was Deputy Lieutenant of Perthshire, while her mother Geraldine Tyssen-Amherst was the daughter of the 1st Baron Amherst. Victoria was named after the Queen herself, who incidentally was her godmother. I believe it's possible that the Drummonds were not short of a bob.

Drummond showed an early interest in marine engineering and at 21 began apprenticing in Perth and then Dundee. Steadily she worked her way up the engineering grades whilst working on passenger and cargo ships bound for Australia, China, Africa and India. But chief engineer certification eluded her, and I suspect it wasn't because she didn't know her spanners.

During the war, the Navy were desperate for chief engineers, hastily bumping up experienced second engineers to meet the demand – but not so desperate as to let a woman do the job. Drummond sat and failed the exam 37 times before obtaining a Panamanian chief engineer's certificate, the exam for which omitted one crucial element: the candidate's gender.

Serving at sea was made significantly more challenging by the antics of the Luftwaffe. Drummond experienced enemy attacks on several occasions and was awarded an MBE for her bravery in 1941. Despite this, it was 1959 before she was regularly employed as chief engineer, by which time she was 65.

Coolness rating: Aquamarine cool

IAN HAMILTON
(Born 1925)
Advocate

A QC and pillar of the establishment for over 60 years, Ian Hamilton is nevertheless best known for one of the most outrageous acts of youthful rebellion in Scottish history. On Christmas Eve 1950, he and three Glasgow University colleagues took student japes to new levels by walking into Westminster Abbey and liberating the Stone of Destiny from its home under the Coronation Chair. You'd think they'd have been happy with a traffic cone.

Also known as the Stone of Scone (pronounced 'skoon', deadbeats) and, on the uptight side of the Scottish border, the Coronation Stone, the Stone of Destiny was used for the coronation of Scottish monarchs for hundreds of years before being plundered in 1296 by Edward 1, who saw it as symbolic of his power over Scotland. It's not known whether Edward was over-compensating for micro genitals, but it's often the way of these things.

Paisley-born Hamilton was part of the university's Scottish Nationalist Association and it's safe to say had strong views about Destiny's incarceration. But managing to get a 152kg slab of red sandstone out of England without anyone noticing was a major triumph of political conviction over the laws of physics.

In April 1951, following an unsuccessful search by the British Government, the Stone showed up on the altar of Arbroath Abbey, famous for its Declaration of Arbroath, the 1320 statement of Scottish independence. Its arrival there may not have been a coincidence.

Needless to say, when the plods found out, it was hauled back to Westminster, but in 1996, after growing dissatisfaction in Scotland with the constitutional settlement, it took up permanent residence in Edinburgh Castle. Hamilton turned down an invitation to the official returning ceremony and it's as well he did, because the Duke of York made it clear that this was strictly a loan from his Mum. I'd have been concerned about Hamilton's blood pressure.

Coolness rating: Destined for cool

As long as only one hundred of us remain alive

EVELYN GLENNIE
(Born 1965)
Percussionist

One of the world's foremost musicians, Glennie is the first person to sustain a full-time career as a solo classical percussionist and is all the more remarkable because she has been profoundly deaf since the age of 12. Musicians are so in awe of her ability that they've stopped telling drummer jokes at parties – which is a great pity, as 'one to change the lightbulb and four to talk about how much better Neil Peart could have done it' still makes me laugh.

Born in Aberdeenshire to farmer parents, her father played the accordion in a Scottish country dance band. As far as I'm aware, no-one has suggested that her deafness was a wilful response to early accordion exposure.

A musically gifted child with perfect pitch (the ability to identify a note by ear and accompany key-changing drunks at parties), her first instruments were the clarinet and piano, but by the age of 8 she began complaining of hearing loss. At 11 she was given a hearing aid, which was quickly discarded, and by 12 she had the severe impairment (but not total deafness) that she has today. On expressing her intention to continue her studies with percussion, her music teacher asked, 'How are we going to do this? Music is about listening.' 'I agree,' she replied. 'What's the problem?'

Glennie was challenging the assumption that listening is something done solely with the ears. She believes that pitch and quality of sound can be experienced from reverberations felt in the hands, arms, lower body and feet, and, in the music of Chris de Burgh, the lower digestive tract. Having a hearing impairment was not going to interfere with her musical development, and probably meant she had to suffer 'Lady In Red' like the rest of us.

Glennie's mission has always been to teach the world to listen. And with over 30 albums and 80 international awards to her name, the world is sitting up and reverberating nicely.

Coolness rating: Profoundly cool

JIMMY REID

(1932–2010)

Trade unionist and politician

The best MP we never had, Jimmy Reid was a powerful speaker who was instrumental in ensuring Scotland still has a shipbuilding industry today but who, having failed to win seats in 1970 and 1979, had limited success in the world of party politics. Some might call his political forays unlucky, but at least he didn't have to spend much time around other politicians.

Reid was born in Govan, Glasgow, and left school at 14, going on to become a shipyard engineer. He gravitated towards the Communist Party but found that gravity works in mysterious ways, later joining the Labour Party, then the Scottish National Party. Ideological flexibility wasn't a problem for Reid but, as he found out, parties of the left don't tend to be big fans of it.

He rose to international prominence in 1971 when the British government decided to stop subsidising Clyde shipbuilding, meaning the yards would close and 6,000 employees could take a permanent unpaid holiday. Reid, by now shop steward of the Amalgamated Union of Engineering Workers, knew a strike would be counterproductive – the government would jump at the chance to lock out the incumbent workers and, being Conservative, would likely do it with glee.

Reid and his colleagues had a better idea: they locked out the management instead. Workers took direct control of shipyard operations, fulfilling the orders that remained on the books and ensuring business as usual. By February 1972, the government were so confused as to how working class people could function without several tiers of bosses, they backed down and agreed to further funding.

It was Reid's compelling rhetoric that captured the world's imagination. In a 1971 speech as Rector of Glasgow University, he said: 'I challenge the right of any man or any group of men, in business or in government, to tell a fellow human being that he or she is expendable.' The *New York Times* printed the speech in full and Conservative politicians everywhere got very nervous.

Coolness rating: Up the workers cool

NAN SHEPHERD

(1893–1981)
Novelist and poet

Between 1928 and 1933, Anna 'Nan' Shepherd wrote three novels which are widely considered to be high water marks in Scottish Modernist literature: *The Quarry Wood*, *The Weatherhouse* and *A Pass in the Grampians*. She never wrote another, and one can only wonder if the experience of dealing with publishers was just too traumatic for her. She certainly seemed to prefer teaching to going near another one, which is really saying something.

Shepherd was born and raised in the suburbs of Aberdeen and, although widely travelled, remained there throughout her life. An avid hillwalker, her main attraction to the area seems to have been the nearby Grampian Mountains, which stretch across almost half of Scotland's landmass. Aberdonians generally can't get very far without bumping into one.

Shepherd's affinity with the terrain was deep-seated and, sometime in the 1940s, she wrote *The Living Mountain*, a non-fiction work of poetic prose that explored her close relationship with the land. It was well before its time; an early example of what we now call nature writing, and all the more unusual for being a female perspective on what was then something you might do only if you sported substantial beardage.

But Shepherd sat on the manuscript for 30 years, presumably reluctant to have another conversation with a publisher, which admittedly can be life-shortening. It was 1977 before she summoned the strength to make that call, and *The Living Mountain* is now regarded as her masterpiece.

In 2016, Shepherd was rewarded for her work and her courage in the face of publishing houses by becoming the first woman to appear on a Scottish £5 note; a surprisingly cool decision by the Royal Bank of Scotland, which is more usually associated with acts of total assclownery.

Coolness rating: Mountain-high cool

KENNY DALGLISH
(Born 1951)
Footballer

Widely considered to be the greatest Scottish footballer of all time, 'King Kenny' is our most capped player, representing his country 120 times and becoming joint-leading goal scorer. As a versatile centre-forward for Celtic and then Liverpool, he won so many cups that visitors to his trophy room are supplied with sunglasses to shield them from the glare.

An engineer's son from Dalmarnock, Glasgow, Dalglish and his family moved to Govan, close to the Ibrox home of the Celts' arch-rivals Rangers, and young Kenneth grew up supporting his local team. After trials for West Ham and Liverpool, an impressed Celtic rep visited him at his parents' home. The 16-year-old panicked. His room was covered in Rangers posters.

By 1971, Dalglish was a regular fixture in the Hoops' first team and over the following five seasons he won four titles, four Scottish Cups and a League Cup, and scored 167 goals. But Celtic, presumably unhappy about goalscoring, decided to transfer him. When Liverpool paid a record fee of £440,000 in 1977, money wasn't so much burning a hole in their pocket as setting their pants ablaze.

At Liverpool, Dalglish was no less impressive. Over the next decade he won three European Cups, six titles, one FA Cup and four League Cups, playing 515 games and scoring 172 goals. In 1985, he became the first player-manager in English football. (A player-manager is someone who manages to play whilst hurling abuse at themselves.)

Generally perceived as a man of few words with a dry sense of humour (a sports editor once called him, asking 'Can you talk?'; he replied: 'I have been known to'), he penned two autobiographies which did their best to dispel his severe image. 'Millions of people who don't know me probably believe I'm a dour Scot,' he wrote. If anything, this just cemented the reputation. It doesn't matter. He was always bright and breezy on the pitch, and that's where it counts.

Coolness rating: King of cool

ISABELLA MACDUFF

(c. 1286–1313)

Countess of Buchan

A significant figure in the original wars of Scottish Independence (long before Westminster claimed Scotland wouldn't get to see *Doctor Who*), Isabella MacDuff was part of the clan traditionally responsible for inaugurating Scottish kings, and personally crowned Robert the Bruce. Details are sketchy (I was unable to find any footage on YouTube), but I have pieced together what is known and used my always reliable instinct to plug the gaps.

Isabella was the daughter of Duncan MacDuff, Earl of Fife, and married John Comyn, Earl of Buchan, making her the Countess of Buchan. Both were influential men; MacDuff was the inspiration for two characters in Shakespeare's *Macbeth*, Duncan and MacDuff; Comyn was the man behind the Robert Burns poem 'Comyn Thro' the Rye'. The latter points may not be true but instinctively feel right to me.

The Comyns and Bruces were two of Scotland's dominant noble families, but following a disagreement involving a drive-by shooting and a drug deal that went badly wrong, the Bruce ended up offing one of the Comyn clan, and in revenge John Comyn sided with the English in the ongoing war.

Isabella texted her husband, saying, 'Have u lost the plot, ya radge?' and he replied with the latest Dunfermline Athletic scores. She took that as a yes, procured some of his horses and men, rode to Scone and planted the royal crown on the noble bonce of Bruce.

Comyn took this act of defiance well. He cliped her to King Edward I, who had her imprisoned in an iron cage outside Berwick Castle for four years. Other than that, it worked out fine.

Bruce eventually had MacDuff freed, and she had no regrets about taking such an active role in helping to ensure that Scotland remained an independent country. With *Doctor Who*.

Coolness rating: Defiantly cool

IAIN BANKS
(1954–2013)
Novelist

Overturning a tradition that authors have observed for centuries, Iain Banks was a genre writer who moved into 'serious literature' in order to make a living. He wrote a total of 27 novels, distinguishing his science fiction from his mainstream work by the inclusion of a middle initial 'M'. Sci-fi fans appreciated the demarcation, as they didn't buy books just to be tricked into reading literature.

The precocious, Dunfermline-born Banks was practically still in the womb when he decided to become a writer. He wrote his first sci-fi novel at 16 and his second at 18, but it was not until he began slumming it in literary fiction that he first had the misfortune to deal with a publisher. *The Wasp Factory* was a wickedly dark and controversial debut, described on its release in 1984 as 'a work of unparalleled depravity'. It sounded brilliant.

After a series of mainstream books, his publisher agreed to release a sci-fi novel, *Consider Phlebas*, under the name Iain M. Banks, although there was some disagreement over who would pay for the extra M. (Publishers are notorious penny-pinchers; they suggested 'Iain I. Banks' to save ink. Eventually they agreed to an M, as long as it didn't have serifs.)

Thereafter, Banks would alternate between mainstream and science fiction, producing a book a year and regularly ranking in lists of greatest British writers. But in 2013 whilst nearing completion of *The Quarry* – a story about the final weeks of a man with terminal cancer – he discovered that he too had an inoperable form of the illness and was given less than a year to live.

He broke the news of his condition in characteristic style, saying online that he was 'officially very poorly' and that he had asked his partner Adele if she would do him the honour of becoming his widow. 'Sorry', he added, 'but we find ghoulish humour helps.'

Coolness rating: Wickedly cool

MARION GILCHRIST
(1864–1952)
Doctor

The first woman to graduate from the University of Glasgow and the first to gain a medical degree in Scotland, Gilchrist battled a system designed to protect those lacking a Y chromosome from the stresses of difficult, intellectual environments and allow them to tend the home and not have to worry about voting. She paved the way for generations of ungrateful women to follow.

Born in Bothwell, Lanarkshire, Gilchrist left school at 13 to work on her father's farm, later attending Hamilton Academy and taking correspondence courses until, by the age of 23, she had reached a university entrance standard. There was only one problem. Entrance was barred to women.

However, the xx-only Queen Margaret College offered the nearest thing to an arts degree for uppity women determined to get above themselves, and by 1890 Gilchrist had bagged one. Not a Bachelor of Arts (BA), or Master of Arts (MA), but a 'Lady Literate in Arts' (LLA), an MA with a less threatening name.

She then enrolled in the newly-created Queen Margaret College Medical School, and in 1894 – by which time it had recklessly been decided that women should be allowed to study and graduate the same as men, and the college had merged with the University of Glasgow – Gilchrist found herself making history.

Unfortunately, being one of the best-educated women in Scotland didn't mean she was allowed to vote, and in 1902 she helped found the Glasgow and West of Scotland Association for Women's Suffrage. Five years later, she still wasn't allowed to vote, and joined the more militant Women's Social and Political Union and the Women's Freedom League.

Gilchrist became a respected ophthalmic surgeon and leading member of the British Medical Association. It was 1928 before women could vote on the same terms as men and incredibly, it was the 1930s before the 'Lady Literate in Arts' was discontinued.

Coolness rating: Doctor of cool

EDUARDO PAOLOZZI

(1924–2005)

Artist

Eduardo Luigi Paolozzi was one of the first and best-known exponents of Pop Art, a movement that confounded art critics by being a hit with normal people.

Paolozzi was the son of Italian immigrants who ran an ice-cream business in Leith, Edinburgh. Unfortunately, his father took a keen interest in the work of Benito Mussolini, an early prototype of Donald Trump, and when Italy declared war on Britain in 1940, he and Eduardo spent three months in Saughton Prison trying to clear up the whole fascist dictator thing. Thereafter, Paolozzi the younger showed great wisdom in never trusting politicians of any hue.

He studied in Edinburgh and London then moved to Paris where he became acquainted with some of the original surrealists. It was during this period that he began working in collage, creating rudimentary combinations of cut-out images from pulp magazines and whatever else came to hand. I can't imagine why anyone would want to do such a thing, but in Paolozzi's hands this slacker pursuit became fine art.

Collage also played a big role in his main medium, sculpture. Classical heads were fused with machine parts and scrap metal to startling effect, the end results suggesting mutated men struggling to come to terms with an increasingly mechanised world. Which brings me back to art critics.

Although his achievements were widely acknowledged, Paolozzi was only represented by a handful of art dealers in his lifetime. It's said that this was due to his 'difficult' personality, but perhaps he just didn't like art dealers. Can we blame him? My motto, 'never trust anyone in a cravat', has always served me well.

Towards the end of his life, Paolozzi donated a large quantity of his work to the Scottish National Gallery of Modern Art. Apart from creating great art, that is just about the coolest thing an artist can do.

Coolness rating: Monumentally cool

MAGGIE BELL
(Born 1945)
Singer

Once hailed as 'the British Janis Joplin', the legendary blues-rock belter could certainly match Joplin in a bawling contest, but crucially knew when she'd had enough Wild Turkey. Bell has sung with Rod Stewart, The Who, AC/DC and Marc Bolan, and it was Led Zeppelin manager Peter Grant's reaction to her voice that saw her band Power renamed Stone the Crows. It's fortunate that Grant was a Londoner, as a more Scottish reaction could have made bookings difficult.

Bell was born in Maryhill, Glasgow, and left school at 15 to become a window dresser. It may not have been the best career choice for someone who could shatter glass from 50 yards, and soon she decided to take her volume out on Sauchiehall Street's Locarno Ballroom instead. Glass was already being shattered there by rival gangs and American sailors, so nobody noticed the difference.

Teaming up with Leslie Harvey, brother of Alex, to form Stone the Crows, the band produced several acclaimed albums between 1970 and 1973, but came to an abrupt and tragic end when Harvey was electrocuted on stage in a freak accident. Bell went solo and signed with Led Zeppelin's newly-created Swan Song label in 1974, going on to tour the US as support for Zeppelin and AC/DC. Both bands said she was excellent, if a bit on the loud side.

In 1981, Bell and B.A. Robertson had a top 20 hit with 'Hold Me', and around the same time she sang the theme songs for hit TV shows *Hazell* and *Taggart*. She even made a guest appearance in the latter, playing the part of a gypsy fortune teller, although hopes that she could become a regular in the series were dashed when the character was murdered ten minutes in.

After 20 years living in Holland, Bell returned to Scotland in 2006, saying enigmatically: 'I met a man and we had a dog. The dog died, so I came home.' Now in her 70s, she continues to perform and has lost none of her coolness.

Coolness rating: Stoney cool

STANLEY BAXTER
(Born 1926)
Comedian

S tanley Baxter is the last of a great generation of Glaswegian TV and stage comics that included Chic Murray, Jack Milroy, Rikki Fulton and Jimmy Logan. He was the first person to impersonate the Queen on television, despite BBC nerves about doing so. It was a brief moment of irreverence in the state broadcaster's otherwise wall to wall royal toadying.

Born in Glasgow's West End, Baxter's father was an insurance manager, a profession not known for its indulgence of young performers, but with his mother's encouragement he became a child star on BBC's *Children's Hour*. He went on to hone his skills during national service alongside Kenneth Williams as part of the Combined Services Entertainment in Singapore. 'They wanted to see women,' he said, 'so that's what we did.' Think *It Ain't Half Hot Mum*.

Moving into television in the 1960s, Baxter performed a series of hugely popular sketches called Parliamo Glasgow, spoofing an Italian language course using the city's unique dialect. ("Izzat a marra on yer barra Clara?" was a favourite.) Revisionist critics have attacked the skits for a perceived condescension, but revisionists are like buses. Any minute a new bunch will come along saying the opposite.

Baxter's golden era was the 1970s. *The Stanley Baxter Picture Show* and annual one-hour specials showcased his talent for mimicry and pastiche in lavish musical spectaculars and spoofs of the big TV shows of the day. The programmes were a massive success, regularly drawing audiences of 20 million viewers, and Baxter was rewarded with... the sack. Always remember that however brilliant you are, some grey drone with a chequebook probably thinks you're too expensive.

A national treasure for many in Scotland, Baxter eased gently into retirement in 1991. It's hard to imagine subsequent Scottish classics like *Rab C. Nesbitt*, *Chewin' the Fat* and *Still Game* having happened without him.

Coolness rating: Parliamo cool

JESSIE M. KING

(1875–1949)

Illustrator

King was one of the leading exponents of the design school known as Art Nouveau, which is French for 'lots of wavy lines and garden fairies'. Art Nouveau should not be confused with Art Deco, Art Moderne or Art Garfunkel. We're talking Willow Tea Rooms rather than 'Bright Eyes'.

Born in the distinctly pan-loafy Glasgow suburb of Bearsden, Jessie Marion King was the daughter of a Church of Scotland minister and had a strict religious upbringing. Her father discouraged her from becoming an artist and forbade use of the word 'pencil'. When, aged 17, his daughter enrolled in Glasgow School of Art and began winning prizes, everyone agreed those years had been a good use of the Reverend's time.

Jessie went on to teach Book Decoration and Design at GSA and married fellow artist E.A. Taylor in 1908. She chose to retain her birth name, which was unusual for the time unless your intended's appellation happened to be Titball, Watmuff or Knoblock.

King established herself as one of the standout illustrators of the period, producing hundreds of designs for everything from book covers to posters. But she also wrote books of her own and was a skilled jewellery and ceramic designer. I believe there is a word for this type of Renaissance figure who displays great expertise in a wide range of subjects. Poly something. Smartarse would do.

Despite commercial success and popularity, by the time of her death, King's whimsical, decorative style had fallen out of favour, possibly due to the emergence of the more fashionable Art Garfunkel school. It was not until the 1970s that the first retrospective exhibitions of her work were held, and since then, critical and commercial favour has steadily increased. Artists who experience this sort of uneven assessment of their careers should always keep in mind that for every period of troubled water, there is usually a bridge.

Coolness rating: Cool nouveau

INDEX

Luath Press Limited

committed to publishing well written books worth reading

LUATH PRESS takes its name from Robert Burns, whose little collie Luath (*Gael.*, swift or nimble) tripped up Jean Armour at a wedding and gave him the chance to speak to the woman who was to be his wife and the abiding love of his life. Burns called one of 'The Twa Dogs' Luath after Cuchullin's hunting dog in Ossian's *Fingal*. Luath Press was established in 1981 in the heart of Burns country, and now resides a few steps up the road from Burns' first lodgings on Edinburgh's Royal Mile.

Luath offers you distinctive writing with a hint of unexpected pleasures.

Most bookshops in the UK, the US, Canada, Australia, New Zealand and parts of Europe either carry our books in stock or can order them for you. To order direct from us, please send a £sterling cheque, postal order, international money order or your credit card details (number, address of cardholder and expiry date) to us at the address below. Please add post and packing as follows: UK – £1.00 per delivery address; overseas surface mail – £2.50 per delivery address; overseas airmail – £3.50 for the first book to each delivery address, plus £1.00 for each additional book by airmail to the same address. If your order is a gift, we will happily enclose your card or message at no extra charge.

ILLUSTRATION: IAN KELLAS

Luath Press Limited
543/2 Castlehill
The Royal Mile
Edinburgh EH1 2ND
Scotland
Telephone: 0131 225 4326 (24 hours)
email: sales@luath.co.uk
Website: www.luath.co.uk